ANTHEMS

General Editor David Willcocks

SATB *a cappella* with organ introduction

O Taste and See

Ralph Vaughan Williams

*Composed for the coronation of
Her Majesty Queen Elizabeth II
in Westminster Abbey
on Tuesday, 2 June 1953*

MUSIC DEPARTMENT

OXFORD
UNIVERSITY PRESS

O Taste and See

Psalm xxxiv, v. 8

R. VAUGHAN WILLIAMS

This motet may be sung in the key of G flat

A version for S.S.A. choir, with organ introduction is also available

R. VAUGHAN WILLIAMS

O taste and see

A 349

ISBN 0-19-353511-4